The Truth about 1

a play

Dentist

Big Teeth — Eye Teeth, Front Teeth, Molars.

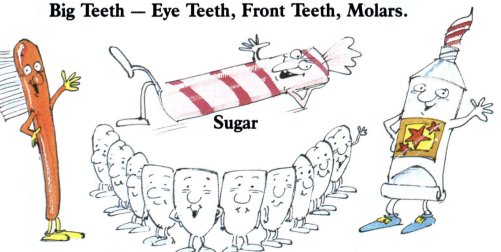

Sugar

Brush   Milk Teeth   Toothpaste

Anna McLeay
Nelson

Dentist
I want to talk about teeth
But it is fair to say
The teeth do it better
In their own way.

Milk Teeth stand in a semicircle.

Milk Teeth
We are milk teeth, oh so small,
We don't grow very big at all.

Brush enters.

Brush
You might be small and very white
But you still need me, morning and night.

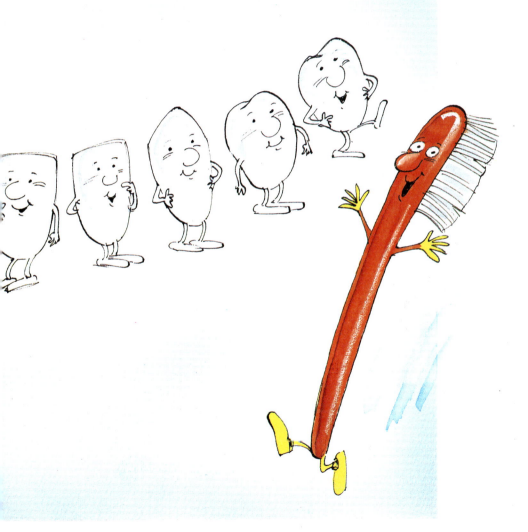

Big Teeth stand behind Milk Teeth.

Big Teeth
>We are the big teeth, tall and stout,
>We push little milk teeth out!

>*Big Teeth push out Milk Teeth.*
>*All Big Teeth form the semicircle.*

Front Teeth
>We are the front teeth, see how we bite
>Big and strong to hold on tight!

First Eye Tooth
>I am an eye tooth, it's plain to see
>You couldn't eat without me!

Other Eye Tooth
>And me!

Molars
>We are molars, see how we chew
>Without us, food is useless to you.

All Teeth
>If we are brushed every day
>You can keep decay away.

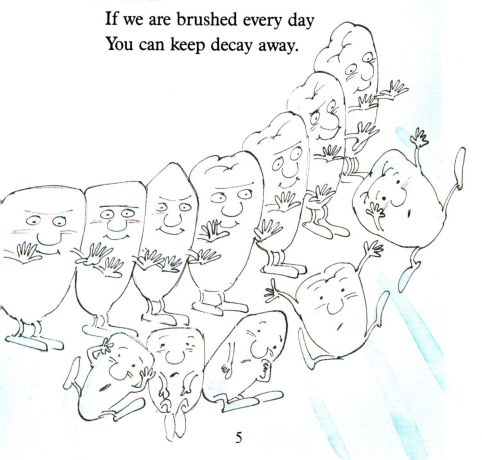

Toothpaste wriggles on.

Toothpaste
   I come out of the tube
   In a great big rush
   I go all over the place
   And miss the brush!

Brush
   Toothpaste and I are here to say
   You need us both, twice a day.
   Toothbrushes get old and frayed
   Get a new one and throw the old one away!

All Teeth scream as Sugar rushes in.

Sugar
   I am the sugar found in sweets
   Children like me in their treats.

All Teeth
   We like chocolate and ice cream
   But the dentist's drill will make us scream!
   Eat a carrot or an apple a day
   Better than sugar in every way!

Dentist
False teeth are not much fun
So come and see me, everyone,
Every six months, and in the end
You will see I am your friend.

Now, how many fillings did I say?

All Teeth
None at all. Hooray! Hooray!